D1324722

Tales from
the "Dalesman"

Dalesman Books
1993

First Published in Great Britain 1993 by
Dalesman Publishing Company Limited,
Stable Courtyard, Broughton Hall,
Skipton, North Yorkshire BD23 3AE
Text © 1993 **Dalesman Publishing Company Ltd.**

Front cover drawing by **Scott Dobson**

ISBN **1 85568 068 8**
Typeset by **Lands Services**
Printed by **Lavenham Press**

All rights reserved. This book must not be circulated in any form of binding or cover other than that in which it is
published and without a similar condition to this being imposed on the subsequent purchaser. No part of this
publication may be reproduced, stored in a retrieval system or transmitted, in any form, or by any means,
electronic, mechanical, photocopying, recording or otherwise, without either prior permission in writing from the
publisher or a licence permitting restricted copying. In the United Kingdom such licences are issued by the
Copyright Licensing Agency, 90 Tottenham Court Road, London W1P 9HE. The right of David Joy to be
identified as the compiler of this work has been asserted by him in accordance with the Copyright Designs and
Patents Act 1988.

Contents

The Daily Round

YEARS AGO, A man called with a N.U.R. contribution, the owner of the house being the local treasurer. The visitor, noted for his long-windedness, prattled on so long into the evening that all began to turn varying shades of pale. He asked: "am noan keeping y' up am a?"

The house-holder retorted: "Nowa, but wis g' t'bed when tha's guan!"

★   ★   ★

AN OLD COUPLE lived in a lonely country cottage. They did not have many visitors as people thought they were "a bit queer".

One day the old woman called to see the local doctor. "I think yer should come and see Fred," she said, "ther's summat wrong wi' 'is ee'seet. When we go to bed at neet, he always says he can see little six-legged pink mice on t'bed."

"He's talking nonsense," said the doctor.

"That's wot I tell'd him," said the old woman, "cos they're breet red."

★   ★   ★

A TRAVELLER WHO visited Dales hamlets and villages had a long white beard. When a customer opened the door to him, her husband, who liked his "liquor" and was snoozing, slightly muddled, by the fire, opened his eyes and exclaimed: "Maggie, there's a hoss backin' in!"

★   ★   ★

A DOCTOR CALLED to see a railway signalman who had been off duty with rheumatism. After examining him, the doctor remarked: "It would be a good thing if you took a bath before you retire."

"Nay," said the signalman, "that's a long time to wait. I don't retire for another 10 years."

★   ★   ★

TWO MIDDLE-AGED ladies at a Doncaster market stall were discussing a third lady who did not find favour with them.

Said one lady to the other: "Eee, she's as miserable as sin! Nivver speaks to anybody, and when she does she says nawt."

THE CITY MAN came out of the village "local" with a pal to walk to their lodgings. There was a weird scream out of the night and the city man jumped.

"What was that?" he gasped.

"An owl," said his pal.

"Yes, I know. But what was 'owling?"

★　　★　　★

IN THE LOUNGE of a North Yorkshire hotel a visitor talked several times to a man who, from the cameras he carried, as well as a mass of other equipment, appeared to be an enthusiastic photographer.

One day after dinner he told the visitor of the day's excursion and said he had met what he thought was the poorest 'down-and-out' he had ever set eyes on.

"Poor old chap," he said. "He looked as if he hadn't a bean in the world and I was really affected by his grim life story."

"What did you give him?" the visitor asked.

"Oh, a hundredth at f.11," said the camera enthusiast.

★　　★　　★

A DOCTOR WHO had a neurasthenic patient said to him: "Say each morning, 'The glorious sun is beating down on me and curing me.'"

A week later the patient reported progress. "I'm much better," he said.

"Good!" replied the doctor, "Keep it up."

After another week the doctor called at the house and was met by the man's wife. "He's very ill," she said.

"Good gracious, what's the matter?"

"Sunstroke, I think," said she.

★　　★　　★

HEARING THAT A man in a Yorkshire village had reached the age of a hundred, the reporter interviewed a neighbour on the subject.

"You must be very proud of him," he remarked. "Oh, I don't know," was the unexpected reply. "The only thing he's ever done is grow old, and he's taken a mighty long time over that."

★　　★　　★

IN A LITTLE Dales town an evening class was studying German. "Now," said the German-born teacher. "Tonight ve vill talk about a railway journey: ve vill start on ze station. Ze German for railvay station is 'der Bahnhof'. Can anyone find a gut vay to remember der Bahnhof?"

"Aye lad, Ah can," said a voice.

Everyone gasped. It was the dunce of the class who had answered.

"Oh yes, Mr X, and just how vill you remember zis vord – zis Barnhof?"

"Well," said the student, "whenever Ah go to t' station, Ah'm allus bahn off somewheer."

The teacher never understood why the whole class roared with laughter.

*   *   *

ASK A BILSDALE man about the weather, and he'll tell you straight: "There's nobbut two soorts o' weather, good and bad."

On a fine day, he'll remark: "We can do wi' this an' better." On a bad day, he'll say: "It'll get worse afore it gits better."

Farming talk usually takes the same pessimistic view.

"How's taties, Joe?"

"Oh why, they cad do wi' some rain."

Same day: "How's t'hay Ted?"

"Why, it wants some yat sun on it, and then it's not as good as last year's crop."

*   *   *

TWO OLD MEN were discussing the respective sizes of their large families.

"Aye," said one, "I'd eleven, all lasses. I'd a' liked a cricket team but Ah gait a sewing class."

7

A MAN WHO was wanted by the police was photographed in six different positions. The pictures were sent to a police chief in a small town where the fugitive was thought to be hiding. After a few days, headquarters received the following message:

"Sir, I have arrested five of the six men whose photographs you sent me. The sixth is under observation and will be secured shortly."

★　　★　　★

A RYEDALE MAN bought a new overcoat and brought it home for inspection. "It looks all right," said the wife, "but it seems queer when you put it on." The new owner looked at himself in the mirror. "It's that fool of a tailor," he said. "He's put a button short at the bottom and one too many at the top."

★　　★　　★

SOME BUILDERS HAD to go to a remote farm to do some work. They sent their youngest "lad" to hire a horse from the next village. After completing the deal, the owner of the horse asked:

"How long will you want it?"

"Oh," said Jack, "we shall want t'longest thoo hes. There's five on us."

★　　★　　★

ABE, A SIMPLE-MINDED youth who did odd jobs for the local blacksmith in a small Yorkshire town, was given an old watch by his employer. One day Abe arrived at the smithy and announced sadly: "T' watch 'as stopped, Mr Cawthra."

"Then we'd better 'ave a look at it, lad," said the blacksmith, removing the back of the watch.

Inside was a small dead fly.

Abe's eyes widened.

"Ee, nooa wonder its stopped," he said slowly, "t' driver's deead."

★　　★　　★

A LEEDS MAN, who has always been in the habit of being last at work, arrived as usual several minutes late the other morning.

"How is it thou's allus t' last?" asked the foreman.

"Somebody's hes to be t'last," replied the man.

"That's reight enough," said the foreman.

"Well, then," replied the latecomer, "thou might as well hev somebody thou can rely on."

THE PROS AND cons of marriage were being discussed with a local bride-to-be. She said: "Marriage is like my mother's clipped mats – you've got ti stick at it till it's finished."

★　　★　　★

THE MANAGEMENT OF a West Yorkshire Co-op Minimarket recently changed, after many years, with the arrival of an enthusiastic, efficient young man, eager to both oblige and impress. Shelves, previously rigid, suddenly bowed and creaked under the enormous weight of goods and bottles displayed thereon.

One of the local veterans inquired gruffly: "hev yu ony leeters?"

"Litres of what?" asked the young manager politely.

"Fireleeters!" came the caustic reply.

★　　★　　★

OVERHEARD IN A Dales teashop, where three farmers were gossiping over tea, their heads nearly touching.

"So I says to 'im, 'Look 'ere, I says, 'you're poorly. You've 'ad all them teeth out and you aren't fit fer to talk business. You go 'ome,' says I, 'and I'll see you when you're really better. For you'll need all your strength for to listen to what I've got to say to you'."

★　　★　　★

FRED WAS HABITUALLY late in turning up for work at a West Riding mill, in days long ago when bosses were present early in the morning to check the men and women through the gate.

One morning, the boss said, gruffly, "Hey, Fred, doesn't tha knaw that t'buzzer's gone?"

Said Fred, without embarrassment: "They'll pinch owt these days."

9

In a Few Words

OUTSIDE A COBBLER'S shop in Thorne, South Yorkshire:
"The Devil wants your souls to ruin; I want them to mend."

★ ★ ★

ON A YORKSHIRE CHAPEL:
"The coming of the Lord draweth nigh. Entrance at the side door."

★ ★ ★

THE VICAR WAS showing the bishop the parish hall.
Bishop: "What kind of heating is it?"
Vicar: "Most peculiar."

★ ★ ★

A DALESMAN HAD a reputation for meanness. His cottage cellar was lit by a dim electric bulb which he switched on at the head of the cellar steps. The cellar was crammed with junk. He had been in the cellar for a long time, searching unsuccessfully for something he was quite sure he had put down there, when his wife shouted down. Could she help him look for it? "Nay lass," came the reply, "light bill will be big enough wi' out two of us being dahn here wasting electricity."

★ ★ ★

SAID A LONDONER to an old villager in his cottage on the cliff top at Kettleness: "There cannot be much fresh air in these old places."
"Young man," replied the native, in his broad Yorkshire brogue, "there's more fresh air comes through our keyhole than you have in all London."

★ ★ ★

A DALES GARAGE mechanic commented to a friend that his new haircut looked fine. "But how much did it cost you?" he inquired.
"One an' sixpence," was the reply.
"Nay," retorted the mechanic. "If you'd paid fer our Bill two or three pints 'e'd ev cut it fer nowt!"

10

**"He caught me using an electric mixer
for the Yorkshire pudding . . ."**

AN OLD MAN annoyed because the blade of his scythe was not properly set: "I don't want to 'eat it," he commented, "for fear it'll lose its temper."

★   ★   ★

A DALESWOMAN REMARKED to the roadman what grey weather there was, saying how cold the outlook was across the valley. He agreed and then his face suddenly brightened and pointing across the valley to the only small patch of sunlight in a field he said: "Aye, but there's a bit ower theer that's slipped 'em."

★   ★   ★

OVERHEARD: Two old countrymen bewailing the increased cost of living these days. One said to the other: "It's a dear do deeing terday."

ON AN OLD bachelor being asked how his new housekeeper was suiting him, he answered: "Wia! I'll tell thee what it is: she's bin a roamer, and she's garm (going) ta he' ta roam again."

★　　★　　★

HEARD IN A Dales bus:
Elderly woman to another: "Ah see i' t'paper thy Sarah's getten t'precious gift of a son."
Other woman: "That's reight. But Ah've telled her, 'Thee wait till tha's getten twelve precious gifts, same as thi Ma!"

★　　★　　★

AT THE BEATERS' dinner, they were boasting of the size of the mushrooms they had gathered. Dick Eastwood, of Threshfield, capped them with: "Ah've a cross-cut fast i' one dahn at hoame!"

★　　★　　★

OLD MARIA CALLED me in to see her new kitten. "Look," she said, "it sits so nice in front of the fire and curls its tail round just like a Christian!"

★　　★　　★

AT A MEETING of our District Nursing Association the proposed gift of a stretcher was announced.
"Yes, indeed," said our President, "I feel most strongly that we ought to have a stretcher in the village to fall back on."

★　　★　　★

MEMBERS OF THE village youth club went for a holiday in Göttingen, Germany, during last summer. The visit was arranged on an exchange basis and the youth club members were to stay in the homes of teachers who had been given reciprocal hospitality in England.
On nearing Göttingen and whilst preparing to leave the train, one of the youths remarked: "Well, Ah 'opes ma 'ost kon speaak English."
"Aye," said his companion, "Ah 'opes 'e kon, cos thoo can't."

★　　★　　★

AN OLD YORKSHIREMAN was holding forth on the merits of being a bachelor. He said: "I allus liked warkin' wi' wimmen, but I nivver wanted to wed yan; they cost too mich to keep."

12

". . . today – gave up smoking!"

A SIGN WRITER was asked to paint a sign for the pub *Hare and Hounds*. When he had completed the customer complained because there was too much space between "Hare and and and and and Hounds!"

★　　★　　★

THE LATE Dr. Hambley Rowe (Cornishman by birth, Yorkshireman by adoption) used to tell the story of a doctor who attended a Yorkshire baby, who wailed bitterly as soon as he set eyes on him. The mother said tactfully: "Tha mun tak' no notice o' t'bairn, doctor. He wor once freetened by a man wi' a fahl face."

★　　★　　★

OVERHEARD on Whitby Quay: "Aye an' t'roak (mist) woar that thick, that if we 'adn't knawn where we wore, we wouldn't 'a knawn where we wore."

★　　★　　★

THE PARTY WAS discussing whether it was better to be up at crack of dawn and set off early for a holiday or have a few hours extra in bed and go later in the day. An old man in the corner looked up and said: "I think they're idle that can't get up to laik."

"Ah reckon this lad's new to t'job."

SCHOOLMASTER TO SMALL boy: "What does B.C. mean?"
  Boy: "Before Christ."
  Master: "And what does A.D. mean?"
  Boy: "After the Devil."

★   ★   ★

IF YOUR WIFE is away, and you want her to hurry back, just send her a copy of the local newspaper with an item on the front page clipped out. Never fails.

★   ★   ★

ONE MAN TO another: "So far as the wife is concerned it's just a case of mind over matter. She doesn't mind and I don't matter."

★   ★   ★

MY HUSBAND HAD a jobbing gardener working for him, and one day the gardener was working with his coat off. A farmer friend came by and called out: "Get thi cooat an, thou'll starve thi shirt."

SAID BY THE village sage of a very grumbly old lady: "I tell't her she mun think on t'Israelites, out in t'wilderness for forty years – an' it wer all for grumbling."

★   ★   ★

MY SMALL DAUGHTER was being taught to say her prayers. We had got to "Give us this day our daily bread," when she looked up inquiringly and asked: "But who's going to make the tea?"

★   ★   ★

FROM A Visitor's Book: "He was a wise man who made up the alphabet. He put Tea before You, as they do here."

★   ★   ★

OVERHEARD: "Nivver hed sich a job i' mi life. If yer copped swee'atin, yer sacked."

★   ★   ★

AN OLD LADY made a habit of going into the churchyard each day. A friend could not understand why she did this. She was told: "Ah lass, you can't believe what a grand feeling it is to be able to walk out again at eighty!"

★   ★   ★ .

IT WAS IN a Dales drapery shop that I heard one woman say to another: "Dun yer wishens weshen weel?" Which translated means: "Do your cushions wash well?"

Of Tender Years

ONE EVENING SAM'S missus was called away to visit a sick friend, and left Sam to put the family to bed. Most of them were outside, playing in the street.

On her return she went up to the children's room, to check that all was well. "But," she exclaimed in horror, "that boy over there's not one of ours!"

A look of relief crossed Sam's face. "Ah," he cried, "that explains it. I wondered why he howled so when I fetched him in."

★ ★ ★

IT SEEMS THAT humour appears early in Yorkshire! While walking home from school with my five-year-old daughter, we noticed that an enterprising neighbour had placed in his front garden a discarded lavatory pan, presumably with a view to growing plants in it. "I expect they'll be loo-pins," observed Katie seriously!

★ ★ ★

CHILDREN AT A North Yorkshire school watched a swashbuckling, action-packed film about pirates. They were then asked to write an essay on "What their pirate did". My friend's daughter gave this a *great* deal of thought and wrote: "My pirate slept all day Monday. The end."

★ ★ ★

WHEN MY BROTHER was a child his weekly pocket money was often spent, not on sweets, but on bus fares to reach the country for a hike or a "tadpole catching" excursion.

On one of these excursions with his young friend Gordon, the latter's pet spaniel, "Laddie", insisted on accompanying them, in spite of all efforts to dissuade him.

The bus arrived and my brother proffered a sixpence, asking for "two threepenny ones, please."

The conductress punched the tickets and added; "And twopence for the dog."

Gordon, fiercely clutching Laddie's collar, was almost on the point of tears when he replied: "But I don't *want* to sell him."

YOUNG JOHNNY WAS proudly telling his Dad that he had been chosen for the part of an elderly man, 30 years married, in the school play. "Well," said his Dad, "I'm reight disappointed."

"Whatever for?" asked the lad.

"Because I thowt tha'd at least ha' landed a speaking role this year' that's why," grumbled father.

★ ★ ★

A YORKSHIRE FATHER promised his son that if an examination was passed he should have a bicycle as a reward. The boy failed and there was the inevitable inquest.

"Well, tha's lost thi bike. Whatever 'es ta bin doin?" said the father.

Tryin' ter learn to ride," said the son, ruefully.

★ ★ ★

A SMALL BOY went home from school very worried. He told his mother he was known to the other lads as "Big-heead".

"Doan't thee worry, lad," said a comforting mother. "For Ah'm sewer there's nowt in it."

"It's a kind of great, great, great grandfather clock."

THE VICAR WAS visiting the little village school. To test the Scripture knowledge of the pupils he asked: "Now children, I wonder if you can tell me what this means, 'And they were astonished at his doctrine'?"

"Yes, sir," said one small boy. "They were fair capp'd!"

★ ★ ★

AN EIGHT-YEAR-OLD had been taken on a visit to Bolton Abbey and the story of the building and its monks apparently made a deep impression. "But you know," she said as she left the ruins, "those monks have left the place untidy, haven't they?"

★ ★ ★

IT WAS AT a West Riding Sunday School party just before Christmas, when the writer asked little Janet (aged five) what Father Christmas was going to bring her.

"He's going to bring me a new velvet dress."

"And what is he going to bring your John?"

"Oh, John's asked him to bring a television set, but mummy says she doesn't think he will."

★ ★ ★

I ATTENDED THE village school as a small boy and one day sat in class with other nine-year-olds listening dutifully to our schoolmaster. He was giving us a talk on the workings of the post office and how our letters, etc., came to be delivered to their correct addresses. It was an interesting lesson and I, for one, enjoyed it.

As was usual at the end of a lesson the schoolmaster asked questions of us to ensure we understood what he'd been talking about. Pointing to one boy on the front row of the class, the master said: "Did you get any mail this morning, Tommy?"

"Yes, sir," Tommy Morgan replied. "Two sacks."

"What," said the master, "you received two sacks of mail this morning?"

"Yes, sir," said Tommy, "for t'pigs!"

★ ★ ★

A SCHOOL PARTY had been into the village on a coach trip and the talk in the local turned on to modern life and education.

"Nay," said one old fellow in the corner as he leaned over to a man who could have been forty years younger, "we make nowt of eddication up here, lad. We uses our brains instead."

THE SCHOOLTEACHER FROWNED at little Agnes. "It's butter, dear – not bootter," she said.

Little Agnes puzzled it out for a moment. Then she put up her hand. "What dear?" asked the teacher.

"Please miss," said the little girl, "what do I say for jam?"

* * *

DURING A SPELL of bad weather, my neighbour decided to take her children's mid-day meal up to school to save them the trouble of trudging home through the snow.

She packed a nourishing dinner into her basket and delivered it safely to the two favoured ones.

Half-an-hour later young Sheila burst into the house with the empty dishes. "Here you are, Mum," she said. "I know you hate leaving dirty pots."

* * *

TWO YOUNGSTERS BOARDED a Wharfedale bus. The bigger of the two asked for a "Thruppence-hawpenny coomback."

"Tha wants a wot?" asked the conductor.

"Thruppence-hawpenny coomback," the lad repeated.

"I suppose tha wants t'same," the conductor said to the smaller lad. "Nooa," was the reply, "I want a tuppenny stop theer."

* * *

A MOTHER REMARKED to her small son: "Your hands are very clean today for a change. What has happened, John?"

"Oh, I've been practising whistling with my fingers, mam," was the reply.

* * *

I WAS STAYING at a Dales house a few years ago when the small boy of the family rushed into the drawing room to his mother carrying a dead rat by the tail.

"Oh mother," he cried excitedly. "We've had a heck of a time killing this rat. We biffed him, and hit him, and whacked him with a stick, and then – (here he noticed for the first time the Vicar who had dropped in for tea) – and then God called him home!"

Out of the Mouths . . .

THE JUNIOR CLASS, in a small village school at the foot of the Pennines, was studying spelling. The teacher was explaining how the letter Q is always followed by the letter U.

Examples were flowing freely, and the word "quoit" was given.

"Anyone NOT know what a quoit is?"

The class looked vague. "Michael," said the teacher, "fetch me a quoit."

Off went Michael, proud and pleased to be chosen – and returned triumphantly – with his gaberdine mac.

★   ★   ★

MANY YEARS AGO, when Sunday was a "Holy Day", my young nephew was in Sunday School class. It was a really hot day, and the doors and windows were opened wide but he could not stop fidgeting.

His teacher, in desperation, asked him what his dad would say if his horses "lolloped about like that!"

Quick came the reply: "Nowt, if it were Sunday."

"Funny how you never see any animals on these Nature Trails . ."

SOME MONTHS AGO I took my day-school class on an outing to Fountains Abbey. Most of the boys had never been very far from Hull and went into the grounds of the Abbey excitedly, never having seen anything like it.

One lad – standing near me in the midst of the ruins – looking round in mouth-open awe, said: "Say mister – Ooo brok it?"

★   ★   ★

AFTER GIVING A lesson on building to a class in a Yorkshire school, the teacher, seeing Johnny hadn't been paying much attention, asked him if he could give three different examples of types of windows usually found in houses. After a quick thought, Johnny replied, "Yes sir. Oppen, shut and brokken."

★   ★   ★

A PARSON SAW a boy smoking. He said: "Do you know where little boys who smoke go to?"

The boy replied, "Aye, up t'ginnel."

★   ★   ★

THE TEACHER HAD stressed the need to watch for catches when answering general knowledge questions. Imagine her surprise when the answer to the question "Where does one find elephants?" presented by one bright pupil was: "The elephant's such a big animal it nivver gets lost and doesn't need finding."

★   ★   ★

A VILLAGE SCHOOLTEACHER was instructing a class on the various months of the year. When she came to March, she asked: "What is it that comes in like a lion and goes out like a lamb?"

The reply was unexpected. A small boy on the front row said: "My dad."

★   ★   ★

LIKE MOST LITTLE lads in the old days, feeling desperately hungry, he walked into a grocer's shop and asked for a half penn'orth of broken biscuits. The kind old lady filled the proffered cap with broken cream biscuits.

Looking wistfully at him she handed back the halfpenny. He looked up at her, and said, "Another half-penn'orth, please."

A CHILD WAS brought out by his teacher for a little individual attention on "Numbers". "Now if I had eight nuts in a bag," she said, "and I gave you four, how many would I have left?"

After some hesitation came the reply "Haaf a bag full."

★　　★　　★

A SCHOOLTEACHER WAS trying to impress some Roman history into her class. "Who was Agricola:" was one question, and a bright spark answered: "A drink for farm workers."

★　　★　　★

A DALES TEACHER had punished Tommy so often for talking during school, and the punishment had been so apparently without effect, that as a last resort she decided to notify Tommy's father of his son's fault. So following the deportment mark on his next report, there were these words: "Tommy talks a great deal."

In due time the report was returned with his father's signature, and under it was written:

"You ought to hear his mother."

★　　★　　★

CATHERINE WAS HAVING difficulty in getting to sleep one night. She shouted for her mother. After providing a drink of water, mother told her to count sheep when she was restless.

In the morning, Catherine was asked if she had managed to fall asleep by counting sheep. "No, mummy," replied Catherine sleepily. "I reached 122 sheep, but I couldn't get to sleep because of trying to remember which number came next!"

★　　★　　★

AFTER THE SCHOOL holidays, a boy came home and told his Grandfather that he had been promoted.

Grandad: "How do you mean promoted?"

The lad sighed: "I have been moved to a higher form."

Grandad: "What are your new classmates like?"

Boy: "Champion. We have a coloured boy in the class."

Grandad: "Indeed, what nationality is he?"

Boy: "He's a Pakistani."

Grandad: "Do you know where Pakistan is?"

Boy: "No, but it can't be far away. He goes home for his dinner."

AT A DALES school at the end of the year a teacher set his class of sixteen-year-olds a test. Apparently it was a stiff test – too stiff for one pupil who looked at the paper for half an hour, then shrugged his shoulders and wrote across it: "God knows, I don't. Merry Christmas." He then walked out.

When the results were up on the notice board at the beginning of the new term opposite his name was written: "God passed, you didn't. Happy New Year."

★　　★　　★

A CLASS WAS being told about Jacob and the ladder he dreamed about, when he pictured angels ascending and descending.

"Please miss," said a small boy, "why did yon angels have to climb when they've getten wings?"

"Don't be so daft," said a little girl, "they must have bin in t' moult."

★　　★　　★

A LAD IN the village had a reputation for using bad language. One day his mother saw the policeman and asked him to call at the house and tell him off. The policeman knocked on the door. Young Billy answered it.

The policeman said: "I hear thou's been swearing again. As thou knows, it's again the law."

"Who told thee about it?"

"Nivver mind who told me; a little bird told me."

"A little bird! An' I've been feeding the little blighters all winter."

★　　★　　★

A SCHOOLBOY, BEING naturally taciturn, refused to speak when he attended his new school, and a succession of teachers, psychologists, speech therapists and psychiatrists were of no avail.

One day, at school dinner, he spoke out. "This Yorkshire puddin's terrible," he said. His teacher was overjoyed, but his headmaster was puzzled. "Why have you not spoken before?" he said. "Well," said the lad, "up to now t' Yorkshire puddin's been aw reet . . ."

★　　★　　★

A DAUGHTER RETURNED from a visit to the dentists and after some enquiries remarked that she was certain it was not painless.

"Why," I said, "did he hurt you?"

"No, but he didn't half yell when I bit his finger."

ONE WET PLAYTIME at school, Michael fell over in the playground. He came into school wet-through and covered in mud. The teacher went to his assistance. "Michael – however did you manage to make such a mess of yourself?" she asked. Michael replied: "Twas easy, miss."

★　　★　　★

A TRAVELLING MUSICIAN visited towns and villages in North Yorkshire playing his harp. My small nephew, aged about three or four, ran in to tell his mother: "Come, look mummy. Man outside playing band on railings."

★　　★　　★

IT WAS IN the days when most girls wore pinafores. A small girl went into my sister's house at Bramley, near Leeds. Holding up her pinafore she said, "Look, I have teared mi pinny."

My sister said to her, "You should say 'I have torn my pinafore."

After a moment's pause the small girl looked up and said, "You must be able to say it three ways then, cos I have riven it an' all."

★　　★　　★

TOMMY AND HIS mother were walking along the sea front.

"What's that over there, Mummy?" he asked.

"That's a lighthouse." exclaimed his mother.

"What's it for:"

"To keep the ships from getting on the rocks."

There was a short pause then Tommy said: "We ought to get one for Daddy."

★　　★　　★

MY LITTLE GRANDDAUGHTER has been watching cricket all her four years. Last summer she was with her mother when the open golf tournament was being shown on television. She was watching so closely that her mother said: "Do you like golf, Joanna?"

Joanna said, rather unsurely: "Yes, but that birdie hasn't come out of the hole yet."

Urban Experiences

A DALES FARMER arrived in Leeds on business and, wishing to pay a visit to Roundhay Park, he boarded a tram in City Square.

When the conductor came for his fare, the old farmer said: "Roundhay Park, please."

"Sorry sir, but this tram is going the wrong way for you," said the conductor.

"Well, doan't tell me abaht it, goa tell t'blinkin' driver," was the fiery retort.

★   ★   ★

AT A CERTAIN pub in Sheffield in the old days beer was twopence a pint. But you could get seven pints for a shilling! A stranger came in one evening and, learning this, threw down his shilling. "This is wheer we save summat," he observed.

Going home in the dusk later he found his wife sewing with two candles lit. "Well, Aw nivver did," he exclaimed. "Aw've been saving brass on mi beer, an' tha's been using two cannles!"

And in a fit of righteous indignation, he swept one of the candles off the table!

★   ★   ★

A CHIROPODIST FRIEND tells a very amusing story of one of his clients who has grown old and tired but still retains her old spirit of fun.

When working on the old lady's feet one day, she surprised him by saying in a loud voice: "Ah'll tell thi wat, mister! When ye get older yer feet get farther out ut gate,"

My friend laughingly agreed and sympathised with the old lady, promising to help her all he could in her difficulties.

★   ★   ★

TALKING TO A Londoner who knew little of Keighley, Alderman Joseph Denby was asked: "I suppose you have a very large estate up in Yorkshire. Do you find it difficult to administer?"

"Nay," said the Alderman, whimsically. "I don't know that I do, except that sometimes t'lads leave t'gaate oppen and let t'deer out."

"Of course it's expensive – giant bonsai trees are very rare."

A GENTLEMAN WAS entering the offices of a certain manufacturer just as man came flying down the stairs at breakneck speed.

"Is there something the matter:" he asked anxiously.

"Summat matter? Ah sud just think there is. Ah'm just rushin' off ter t'undertakkers. T'boss es just been takken poorly upstairs."

"But my dear man, you don't want the undertaker. You want the doctor."

"Doctor be blowed; we doan't believe i' middle men at this shop."

★ ★ ★

A WEST RIDING firm advertised for a boiler firer. Joe Longbottom applied and saw the manufacturer.

Said the latter: "We want a gooid man, tha knaws. Tha'll 'a ter be 'ere at fahve ivvery morn, and git thi wark done whether t'foreman' back's turned or no. Tha'll git awf-an-ahr fer thi breakfast, awf-an-ahr fer thi dinner an' tha'll knock off at six after tha's seen 'at ivverything's i' order. It's a big job an' we want a gooid man fer it."

"An' ah mich will Ah git fer doin' all this like?" asked Joe.

"Fahve an' twenty bob a week."

"Aw aye, an do Ah 'ave ter bring mi awn coil wi' me an' all?"

26

A YORKSHIREMAN HAD been invited to spend a week with a friend in London. Off he went, and the week lengthened into a fortnight. At the end of that period, the Tyke decided to return to his native county. The London friend went to the station to see his guest off and on arrival there they decided to have one last drink together. As they entered the buffet, the Londoner put his hand into his pocket to pay for the drinks.

"Sithee 'ere, owd lad," said the Yorkshireman, "tha's been good enough to keep me' an' pay for all mi' drinks this last fortneet, an' Ah think it' time Ah did summat. Ah'll tell thee wot we'll do – we'll toss fer it."

★   ★   ★

A LEEDS PLUMBER was having trouble getting his money from a customer. Four requests for payment had been ignored.

Then the plumber sent another invoice. Across it he wrote: "Man is dust. Dust settles. Be a man!" A cheque came by return of post.

★   ★   ★

AN OLD COUPLE went to spend the day with their daughter and she wanted them to stay overnight. "Nay," they said, "we'll get t'last 'bus home." But they missed the 'bus and had to return to their daughter's home.

Later, the old lady was brushing her grey hair in the bedroom. "Well, though I've got winter in mi hair, I've summer in mi heart," she said.

"Aye," said her husband, "An' if tha had spring in thee feet we'd have got that 'bus."

★   ★   ★

DURING THE WAR years, in a certain Yorkshire district, the knocker-up failed in his duties, and one chap, late for work, was admonished by the foreman, who asked him if he had not got an alarm clock.

"Ah hevn't," he replied. "Ah've a knocker-up. But if ahr knocker-up can't knock fowk up better ner he is dewin', Ah sal hev ta find a knocker-up 'at can knock ahr knocker-up up."

★   ★   ★

HAVING REACHED THE age of sixty, Joe, a Huddersfield weaver, could no longer see to do his work, and his wife was greatly distressed at this state of affairs. Then one day he came home and said: "Buck up, lass, Ah've getten a job as a neet watchman."

His wife burst into tears. "Well, if that isn't t'limit," she sobbed, "just when Ah've made thee two new neet-shirts."

TWO YORKSHIREMEN HAD taken rather too much to drink. As they stumbled along a country road, they had a heated argument about what they saw in the heavens.

One asserted it was the sun. The other was equally certain it was the moon.

Seeing another man approaching, they appealed to him.

One of them said: "Ah say, mister, isn't that t'sun?" The other chimed in, "Nay, it's mooin, isn't it?"

Not wishing to be involved, he replied: "Well, to tell yer t'truth, Ah'm a stranger i' theeas parts."

★ ★ ★

WALTER MORRISON, M.P. for the Skipton Division, felt that he had been libelled by the Liberal Newspaper, *The West Yorkshire Pioneer*. He consulted his solicitor and election agent, Richard Wilson, and it was decided to bring an action in the High Court. When this was down for hearing in London, Mr. Wilson, along with his witnesses, travelled to London and put up at the Inns of Court Hotel in Lincoln's Inn Fields.

On the evening before the trial, Mr. Morrison provided a dinner at the Holborn Restaurant at which after the Loyal Toast the guests were asked to drink "success to our cause". For these toasts champagne had been provided. Later the waiter came round asking everyone what he would now like to drink. One guest, Jack Metcalfe, of Threshfield, replied: "I'm not changing. That bubbly lemonade is good enough for me."

Next morning about six o'clock Jack appeared at his bedroom door with sleeves rolled up and neck and chest bare, demanding of a startled chambermaid: "Na lass, whar's kitchen?" "Kitchen? It's downstairs; but what do you want with it?" "Why to wash mysel. What's tha think?" replied Jack.

★ ★ ★

THE ORGANIST AND choirmaster who served the West Riding church faithfully for well over twenty years was a real old Yorkshire character. He was a fine musician, although self-taught, and he spared no pains to see we had a very good choir.

When the choir was rehearsing Stainer's *Crucifixion* the conductor made the members sing a difficult passage time and time again until he was satisfied it was near perfect.

"Nah then lads," he said, "let's heve 'Fling wide the Gates' ovver just once agean – and think on, doan't hod 'em oppen sa long."

TWO BROTHERS WERE scrap merchants in Leeds. One of them was converted to Methodism. His brother declared that afterwards he was an altered man. His whole way of life changed, not only privately and in his social relations but even in his business.

"He started trying to convert me," he said, "and, by gum, he nearly did it. But then I thought 'Nay. If both of us are converted, who's going to weigh t'scrap?' So I wasn't."

★   ★   ★

WHEN LEEDS WAR Memorial was unveiled a great crowd gathered. An elderly lady collapsed and with a good deal of difficulty was carried through the crowd by two St. John Ambulance men. Then the patient suddenly recovered. "I'm all reet now, lads," she told her bearers, "but tha knaws I'm over seventy, an' it wor the only way I could get to the front."

★   ★   ★

TWO YORKSHIREMEN TRUDGED from Leeds to London. Utterly worn out and thoroughly dejected they limped into Barnet, only to learn that they had still another ten miles to go.

"It's noa use, Bill," groaned one, sitting by the roadside and caressing his aching feet. "Ah'm dead beat, lad. Ah'll nivver tramp another yard, Ah tell thi."

"Dang it," replied Bill, "tha mun stick it somehow. Wheer's thi courage, lad? We'll go on, thee an' me – efter all, it's nobbut five mile apiece!"

Food and Drink

HE ONCE CALLED at a village inn and met an old farm worker he had not seen for many years. As they chatted, a young couple entered. He asked her: "What will you have, darling?" She replied: "Gin and tonic."

The old man nudged Leslie Kemp and said: "They're not married." When asked how he knew, he said: "If they had been, he would have bought her a half shandy, and there'd be no 'darling'."

★   ★   ★

MY FATHER-IN-LAW lived at Hollin Head, Baildon. When he was a boy, he walked with his older brother to see a relative at Guiseley. On being offered a "new cake" to eat on the long walk home, my father-in-law said: "No thank you." His brother said: "Yes, please."

As his brother was enjoying the cake on the way home, my father-in-law's mouth watered. "Give me a bite," he said.

"Nay John, I'll teach you to say 'no thank you' when you mean 'yes, please'."

★   ★   ★

OLD BILL LIKED his ale, but on returning home after a "session" he was always on the receiving end of his wife's whiplash tongue. One night he decided to give her a fright.

He went upstairs, painted his face with flour and lay on the bed as if dead. On seeing him, his wife said: "By gum, Bill, tha looks a lot better deead ner ever tha did when tha wor alive."

Bill jumped up and retorted: "Well, if that's all tha thinks abaat me, ah'll nivver dee ageean as long as ah live."

★   ★   ★

AN OLD MAN, living alone in his small cottage was very fond of his daily drink at the local inn. After one such visit, he slept rather too late next morning.

His neighbour, at mid-day, asked him about his health.

"I've a shocking head," said the toper. "If I'd known I felt so bad, I wouldn't have woken up so early!"

**"You'd look green if you'd gone from Mars
to Yorkshire in half an hour."**

A VISITOR WAS chatting with a farmer in the doorway of the farm wash-house. Inside, the farmer's son was cleaving down the middle of a suspended, newly butchered pig. It seemed a fairly neat job to me, but his father chided: "Hod on, Jonty, hod on! Thou's going to get both lugs on one side!"

★   ★   ★

A SCHOOL TEACHER asked her class if any of them said grace before meals at home. No-one replied. She directed the question at young Johnny.
"What does your father say before you have tea?" she asked.
Johnny said: "Go steady on the butter, lads; it's half-a-crown a pound."

★   ★   ★

TWO MEN SAT at a table in a small Dales cafe. One was a burly individual, and the other a diminutive man in a bowler hat. They both concentrated on their meal for some minutes, when the little man tapped the other on the arm.
"Do you think you could pass the sugar?" he asked timidly.
The burly man scowled. "Ah reckon Ah could," he said. "Ah've been movin' pianos all me life."

31

ON A SUMMER day, a rambler entered a Dales country inn, bought a pint and took a seat in the snug, which was occupied by three grey-bearded dalesmen.

After 10 minutes silence, the rambler suggested that the weather was kind. A further 10 minutes silent cogitation was broken by: "Aye, but ah reckon it'll rain tomorrow," from one of the dalesmen.

Ruminating on this bold prophecy for 10 more minutes, the second dalesman peered through the window and announced "Nay, ah reckon it'll keep up."

The third dalesman, after a similar time-lapse, emptied his glass, rose to his feet and announced: "Ah'm bahn. Can't stand all this 'ere argyfying."

★　　★　　★

"WHY TED!" THEY said as he entered a public bar of a Riccall inn, "thoo's 'ed thi teeth oot. What's t'reason for that?"

"It's t'onny way they could stop me fra biting me nails," replied the poker-faced Ted.

★　　★　　★

WHEN I CALLED at a motorway service station for refreshment I saw a lorry driver I knew sitting at a table.

"Hullo, Jim," I said. "What have you got there – tea or coffee?"

"Nay," replied Jim sadly. "They didn't say."

★　　★　　★

A YORKSHIREMAN ATTENDED a convention in New York. On returning to his remote Yorkshire village, he was seen with his suitcases by an elderly lady, and the following conversation ensued:

"Been away?"

"Yes."

"Been far?"

"New York."

"Makes a change."

★　　★　　★

LITTLE MARGARET WAS helping her mother in the kitchen after breakfast one day in winter. "Dear me," said her mother, "what a very dark morning it is. I don't think it is ever going to be light today."

"I don't think so either, mummy," said Margaret, adding simply: "I guess that God can't find His matches."

32

A MOTORIST WHO stopped for a drink at a wayside pub in Yorkshire was surprised to see that a dog of a native wore brown boots. "Brown boots for a dog," he exploded. "But why?" pressed the visitor.

The native offered to answer the question if the visitor would buy him a pint, and after a bit of quibbling the visitor agreed to do so. "He's wearing brown boots," the native at last explained, "because I've had to take his black 'uns to be mended."

      ★   ★   ★

WHEN ONLY THE larger towns boasted fish and chip shops, two men living in a remote valley went on a trip to Leeds. They saw people buying fish and chips and coming out of the shop eating them, so decided to try some.

The assistant put fish and chips in a paper packet, and the two men walked out into the cold night air and began to sample the delicacy.

"Hey, Jack," said one after a short silence. "These chips taste like 'taties!"

33

TWO YORKSHIREMEN, Bill and Tom, were in a lodging house. Bill gave Tom a sheep's head to boil. Tom put it in the pan and let it boil dry. Bill returned to find Tom kicking the sheep's head around the room saying, "The ruddy thing's supped all t' broth."

★ ★ ★

THE LANDLORD OF a public house, anxious to send some liquor a few miles away, inquired of the local carrier who was a teetotaller, if he would carry it for him.

"Nay," said the carrier, "Ize nut carrying t' divel o' that way. He mun walk it."

★ ★ ★

THEY WERE HAVING a typical Lakeland farmhouse tea and were joined by some Yorkshire youths, who shared their table.

After sampling a large helping of rum-butter one of them leaned across to the other and said: "This honey's a bit off. It tastes to me of rum."

"Christmas shopping makes me feel so tired."

OLD JOHN, HURRYING towards the railway station, was overtaken by a younger neighbour.

"Hey Fred," he called, "will ta book me a return ticket?"

"Wheer to?" asked Fred.

"Back 'ere, yer fooil," replied John.

★　　★　　★

IT WAS A slow train from Hellifield to Leeds. At one small station, a large lady entered and commenced this happy soliloquy:

"Well, I've been wheer they buried 'em with 'am. I've been wheer they buried 'em wi' potted meat (sniff)! But I've nivver been afore wheer they buried 'em wi' roast duck and green peas."

★　　★　　★

A QUARRYMAN WENT into the local shop with an order from his wife.

"Ah want a pound o'butter, four ounce o'tea, four ounce o'yeast an' a stoan of flour. How much?"

"Let's see," said the grocer, "flour's two an' ten a stone an' butter's . . ."

"Two an' ten a stone for flour? 'Afore I'll pay all that, I'll eat dry bread!"

★　　★　　★

AN OLD FARMING couple had been shopping in Halifax. They were boarding the one and only bus back to the village when the conductor informed the farmer that there was only room for one person.

Without more ado, he climbed aboard the bus and, turning to his wife – who was behind him – said, "I'll have a cup o' tea waiting for thee when tha gets home!"

★　　★　　★

A LITTLE GIRL from a remote Dales farm was taken by a friend to a Harrogate cafe and was offered some chocolate sponge, something she had not seen before.

She refused it by saying: "No thank you. Mummy doesn't like me to eat dirty cake."

Business Dealings

WE WERE HOT and very thirsty as we walked across the moors. Then we thankfully sighted a remote farm with the word "teas" displayed on the front.

The farmer was standing by the gate.

"Tea for two," we clamoured.

"Nay! We doan't mak teas."

"But it says you do."

"That wer't chap as lived here afore."

"Oh, well, you must get it off before Easter and Whitsun, or you'll be having a constant stream of inquiries."

"Ah know, we had last year and t'year afore."

★　　★　　★

A LONDONER WATCHED a local blacksmith making a wrought-iron gate. The Londoner said: "It's nice to see a true craftsman at work. I work in the small instrument field were I've got to be accurate to 1/10,000th of an inch."

The blacksmith looked at him and said: "Wheel, in that case thoo'd better stay and watch. Ah's exact."

"In wet weather, this ford is almost impassable . . ."

A YORKSHIRE INSURANCE broker was asked to add a violet mink coat to a client's policy. When the insurance company's reply came, he could scarcely believe what he read. Their memo said: "An endorsement is being prepared for your client's violent mink."

★ ★ ★

A YORKSHIREMAN GOING from York to Liverpool arrived at York station booking office. He asked for a single ticket to Liverpool.

The booking clerk threw the man the ticket, saying: "Change at Leeds." The Yorkshireman quickly replied: "Ah'll ev it noo, if yer dean't mind!" And he held his hand out for the change.

★ ★ ★

A FARMER'S WIFE went into a picture dealer's and asked to see a still life. Eventually she chose one representing a bouquet of flowers, a plate of ham and a roll.

"How much?" she enquired.

"Twenty-five shillings. It's very cheap."

"But I saw one just like it the other day for fifteen shillings."

"It couldn't have been as good as this, madam."

"Indeed, it was even better. There was a lot more ham on the plate."

Home Truths

WHEN VISITORS CALLED, my father would answer the door saying: "Come in. Make yourself at home. I wish you were."

★ ★ ★

A VISITOR TO Yorkshire was taken to Hull and shown the cranes and ships. He said they were very good, but his boy at home built cranes with his construction set bigger than some of those on the docks.

He was taken to see the foundations of the Humber Bridge being laid. He said they had horses that could jump that narrow stretch of water.

He was taken to Flamborough Head, and he asked what it was used for. The Yorkshireman taking him around said: "To measure some of our visitors for their cap size."

★ ★ ★

A HUDDERSFIELD WOMAN had a son not quite as bright as he might have been. She set him to collect loose slates and tiles lying about the garden, and to lay them to form a path. He soon picked up all he could find and for a time work stopped, for he couldn't find any more.

Later on his mother saw him bringing lots more slates and went out to ask him where he was bringing them from. "Oh! From th'roof o th'outhouse," he replied, "and there's plenty more. They are all o'er-lapping up theeer."

★ ★ ★

MRS MOORE HAD 12 children and was about to produce her 13th. "And what are you going to call the new baby?" asked the doctor. Mrs Moore replied: "I shall call him No'ah (Moore)."

★ ★ ★

A FARMER IN the village asked his son to fetch one of the two horses from the field and harness it to the trap to take him to Barnsley.

"Which horse shall I fetch, dad?" asked the boy.

"Bring t'oldest lad," said his father. "We'll use t'oldest up first."

"If it's a case o' that dad," replied the boy, "I think tha'd better go for it."

"And stop saying: 'It might have been worse'."

OLD JACK WAS a mason and a man of the old school. He ruled his household (wife and daughter) with a rod of iron. They were completely awed by him, as he intended they should be.

One day he decided to sweep the sitting-room chimney. but even though he was *the expert* at these matters he somehow failed to fix the cloth securely across the fireplace. At the first thrust of the brush an enormous load of soot fell, tearing away the cloth and covering Jack inches deep.

He staggered out with only the whites of his eyes visible, and spied his terrified womenfolk fluttering about like agitated hens. Furiously he turned upon them, crying, "And never let me catch you lighting a fire in theer again."

★ ★ ★

A BATLEY MAN found himself in Court as a witness in a cattle dealing case. Counsel was finding him tough.

"Tell me, my good man, are you acquainted with any of the jury?"

"Well, Ah know more'n half on 'em."

"Would you be willing to swear you know more than half of them?"

"If it comes to that," replied the witness. "Ah'm willing to swear Ah know more'n all on 'em put together."

A FISHERMAN AT Filey once consoled me, as I stared mournfully out to sea, having many private worries: "Now then, lad – just remember that t'tide turns at low watter as well as at high."

★   ★   ★

OVERHEARD IN A Yorkshire cafe: "I hope t'new government won't raise t'standard o' living any higher. I haven't caught up wi' t'owd 'un yet,"

★   ★   ★

AT A BLOOD donor session in a Wensleydale village, a young man fainted, leading to the exchange: *First Donor* – "That's funny; he were alright at pig-killing." *Second Donor* – "Aye well, that weren't his blood."

★   ★   ★

THE VILLAGER SAID that rooks use only two kinds of twigs when nest-building. He invited a friend to guess which type. There was mention of oak, ash, birch, beech and others. He replied: "Nay, rooks use bent 'uns an' straight 'uns."

★   ★   ★

A YORKSHIRE FARMER had just bought a horse. The buyer said: "Noo tha's got mi cheque, can you tell me if oot's wrong wi' 'er?"
"Aye, that I can. One thing, she's difficult to catch when she's been on t'grass."
"That's nowt much. Ah'll take a 'andful of oats. What else is wrong wi' 'er:"
"Well, when you've catched 'er she's no good anyway!"
"Oh, I see. Well seein' as tha's been truthful, Ah'll tell thoo summat. That cheque tha's just getten is no good nawther!"

★   ★   ★

IT WAS DURING an exhibition in Wetherby Library. An elderly man entered the gallery and examined each picture minutely with the air of an expert.
"Have you enjoyed looking at them?" asked the assistant.
"Aye, I have that," he said. "I can appreciate summat like this. You could say I was in this line o' business misself."
"Oils or watercolours?"
"Neether," he replied, "I used to be a cake decorator."

DURING THE 1914-1918 War, Joe, a Dalesman, had been on a few days' leave and I asked him on his return to duty how he had enjoyed himself.

"Oh, aw right," he replied, "but I faws out wi' t'mother-in-law."

"Well," said I, "what does that mean?"

"Oo said she'd cut me off wi' a shillin'."

"And what did you say to that?"

"I tow'd her, I get moor than t'others ud get," said Joe.

★   ★   ★

"AH'S BADLY," COMPLAINED Tom, of Dentdale, mournfully. He took to his bed. His wife, Alice, looked solemn.

"Tom," she asked him, "Wheaa does ta want ta bi buried?"

"Ah doan't want ta bi buried," he replied.

"But if tha dees, Tom," insisted Alice, "thoo'll ha ta bi buried."

"Weel," replied Tom thoughtfully, "Tak ma ta Cornwall. I'd like ta bi buried bi t'sea."

"Does ta think Ah's gaan to spend aw' that brass on tha?" exclaimed Alice, indignantly. "Ah'll tak tha ta Dent, where tha come fra', and if tha doesn't settle theer, Ah'll tak tha ta Cornwall."

★   ★   ★

AN ELDERLY YORKSHIRE postman was making his usual delivery of letters in a remote part of the hillside, and on reaching a certain house halted to deposit his mail.

After searching his bag without success he simply turned to the lady of the house and said: "Aye well, it were nowt, nobbut a card to say 'at your Alice isn't coming to her tea o'Sunday."

Just Neighbours

TWO NEIGHBOURS IN a small West Rising village quarrelled bitterly about a party wall. One of them went to a solicitor.

"I'm sorry I can't act for you," the lawyer told him, "because your neighbour has already briefed me. However, I'll give you a letter of introduction to a reliable firm across the street."

Wondering why such an introduction should be needed, the aggrieved householder took the letter home. Steaming it open, he read: "Here are two birds ripe for plucking. You pluck one and I'll pluck the other."

The upshot was that the two neighbours got together and resolved their difference without litigation.

★　　★　　★

TWO MEN HAD been fishing from a small boat on a lake day after day without success. At last they found a spot where they couldn't pull them in fast enough.

As they reached the boat house that evening one of them said: "That was a good catch we had today, I hope you marked the spot."

"Oh yes," replied the other. "I put a cross on the bottom of the boat."

"Don't be silly," retorted the first, "we might not get the same boat tomorrow."

★　　★　　★

WHEN MOTHER GOT word that Uncle Arthur was coming to visit us she was all agog. Uncle Arthur, her black-sheep brother, had made a big fortune in Australia, and she was not without hopes that at some time or other he might get his hand down to the benefit of her family.

"Nah mind thi manners," she said to her seven-year-old son Willie. "Tha mun think on o' all t' things Ah telled thi abaht eytin', an' suppin' an' tek thi cap off when tha cums into t' 'ouse."

Uncle Arthur duly arrived and all went well until tea-time, when peas and chips were served. The sight of Uncle Arthur committing all the table sins he had been warned against was too much for the little lad.

"Ah say mother," piped up Willie, "wot's mi Uncle dewing usin' 'is knife ter eyt 'is peas?"

"Eh, lad," chortled mother, "tha dun't need fret abaht yon. 'E's brass enough ter use a shovel if 'e's minded."

JOHN WILLIE WAS supposed to have a slate loose, but where money was concerned he usually finished up on the right side. Once when a chap had been trying to take a rise out of him, he coolly remarked: "Does tha know, Joe, Ah can make sixpence into a shilling."

"Get away wi' thi, softheead," said Joe. "Ah don't believe thi."

"Ah can. Thee lend me sixpence an' Ah'll show thi."

The sixpence was handed over and John Willie went into a nearby butcher's shop. Returning in a moment or two with a pork pie, he handed threepence change to Joe.

"Hey!" shouted Joe, "What's tha tryin' on? This isn't a shilling."

"Ah nivver said it wor, but Ah've made that sixpence into a shilling, all t'same."

"How's tha meean?"

"Well," said John Willie, "Ah'll tell thi. Tha sees this pie. Nah, that's threepence, isn't it? An' tha's got threepence. An' t'butcher's got sixpence hasn't he? Nah just thee reckon it up."

★　　★　　★

A LITTLE GIRL knocked at the door of a thrifty Yorkshire woman's house and said: "Please, missus, mi mother wants to know if you've done with her peggy stick."

"Ah hev, an' be sure an' tell her it's brokken, an' if she doesn't get it mended Ah sall hev to borrow yan somewhere else next time Ah wash."

"My shepherd was brought up i' France."

MOTHER RULED HER six sons and one daughter with a firm but fair discipline. Pa, a quiet, easy-going chap, was happy to let his wife feed and clothe the family as best she could on the small wage of those days.

Pa developed a realistic philosophy towards life and on one occasion said to my husband (No.6 in the family): "Nay lad, doan't argue with your Ma because y'know she's allus reight even when she's wrang!"

★   ★   ★

ONE OF THE neighbours had been rather ill, and the thoughtful house-wife thought she would like to know how she was getting on. So she told her seven-year-old son to slip round "to ask how old Mrs. Brown is today."

He came back very quickly with the reply: "Mrs. Brown says it's none of your business how old she is."

★   ★   ★

IN A SMALL country town were two chapels, with a good deal of jealous antagonism between them. After much effort one had been able to install an organ. One Sunday morning, soon after the installation, two stewards on duty in the porch hailed two members of the other chapel with the words: "Tha sees we've getten an organ," to which the rejoinder was: "Aye, an' all tha wants now is a monkey." Quick as lightning came the reply: "Aye, an' all you want is an organ."

Right to Reply

IN THE 1930s, while teaching an evening class of building apprentices at Huddersfield Technical College, I used in dictation the word necessarily. A country lad turning to his classmate said: "Aah do they spell it?" Back came the reply: "Ah doan't know. Ah allus put essential."

★   ★   ★

HE LIKED TO go into the Dales for his holidays but had no car, so he tramped the roads, always on the lookout for a good subject for his sketch book. Suddenly there it was – a farmyard with old carts set at various angles.

He needed permission to go into the yard, so he sat on the wall, smoking his pipe and waiting for someone belonging to the farm to appear. Eventually a farm hand came in sight. The artist hailed him: "I say, is the farmer anywhere about?"

"Nay," replied the man, "he's in the fields and won't be back 'til after dinner. What' ta want?"

"Well," said the artist, "I only wanted to ask him if I could come in and paint yon carts."

"Nay, I don't know about that," replied the man, "he nobbut had 'em painted last year."

★   ★   ★

THE YORKSHIREMAN EXILED to London found that the Cockneys he worked with were always teasing him about his accent. The final straw came when one proclaimed: "They're all a bit fick up North, ain't they?"

After a pause, the Yorkshireman replied thoughtfully: "Nay, I don't know so much about that. I was allus taught that t'densest population were in London."

★   ★   ★

A LOCAL WHO was travelling up a Dales line by train seemed to be engrossed in his newspaper. Actually he was absorbing all the conversation.

A townsman in the compartment said, "Why you're reading your newspaper upside down."

The reader retorted, "Onny fool can read it reet side up!"

AN ARGUMENT HAD sprung up about something or other, as was not uncommon, and it became very heated. At last one of the contestants got up in a temper and walked to the door saying: "Oh! I can't talk to a d—d fool."

His opponent who was afflicted with a slight stammer called out: "Here – s'stop – c'come b'back – I c'can.

★   ★   ★

AT A YORKSHIRE stately home which was opened to the public a real old-fashioned Tyke was in charge of the gardens. When visitors saw his roses and dahlias they would ask him how he grew such large blooms. "Manure," he said, "Plenty of manure." Then when the visitors saw his vegetable garden they would ask: "How do you grow such large turnips and cabbages?" His answer, as always, was: "Manure. Plenty of manure."

One day his wife and grown-up daughter were standing near when the old man was talking to visitors. The daughter said to her mother: "I wish dad would say fertiliser to the visitors instead of manure."

Mother turned to her daughter and said: "You leave father alone. It look me twenty years to get him to say manure."

FARM RADAR

"There's a weed in yon field."

46

A FARMER NAMED Swan lived at the village of Askham, near York. When a visitor from the south saw a young lad driving some ducks along the street he asked: "What ducks are they?" The boy replied: "Them's Swans." "No, they're not," said the amused visitor, adding: "Where do they come from?" The boy simply replied: "Askham."

★　　★　　★

A PARROT, WHICH unfortunately was given to using bad language, was owned by two ladies, and the only way to stop the bird talking was to cover its cage with a cloth. This they made a point of doing every Sunday for the whole of the day.

One Monday morning just after the cover had been removed, a knock was heard at the door, and through the window the ladies saw it was the minister from the place where they worshipped. Their first thought was to cover up the bird in the cage, and as the reverend gentleman came into the room where the bird was, a voice from under the cloth was heard to say: "That's been a b—— short week!"

★　　★　　★

IT WAS THE monthly meeting of the Rural Council. The members were discussing the epidemic of whooping cough among children.

The parson, who represented his parish, was complaining bitterly and said that the illness ought to have been cleared up long ago. He did not know what the doctor had been doing to let it drag on so long.

When he sat down, the doctor – who was also the Medical Officer of Health – got to his feet, a little rattled, and said that the epidemic was quite normal. It would die out anytime now. He added that parsons had been trying to put down sin for the past 2,000 years and they had not succeeded yet.

★　　★　　★

AN ARTIST WHO was visiting the Dales saw an old countryman whom he thought would make a good model. So he sent his wife to bring over the man to paint him.

The old fellow hesitated. "Will he pay me well." he asked.

"Oh, yes; he'll probably give you a couple of pounds."

Still the old man hesitated. He took off his shabby cap and scratched his head in perplexity.

"It's an easy way to earn a couple of pounds," the lady prompted.

"Oh, I know that," came the reply. "I was only wondering how I'd get the paint off afterwards."

"You're the slowest painter I know, Fred."

AS A SATISFIED customer left our Ryedale Folk Museum, he said: "A wonderful collection. I've used everything you have there!"

After he'd departed, someone at the desk said: "And what did you use the flints for, Methuselah?"

★　　★　　★

A MEMBER OF the amateur operatic society, on being asked how 'Goodnight Vienna' was going down in Batley, replied: "Oh, about as well as 'Goodnight Batley' would go down in Vienna!"

★　　★　　★

HAVING RECENTLY BECOME engaged I took my fiancee to be introduced to my grandmother shortly before the old lady's death at the age of 95.

My fiancee, being urban-bred could not understand my grandmother's greeting, which I interpreted as an expression of pleasure at meeting a prospective granddaughter-in-law.

What the old lady really said was: "Ah see tha's browt thi woman wi thi."

A LADY ONCE asked William Temple, when he was Archbishop of York, if he believed in "special providences". He replied that he could only judge in individual cases.

The lady then told him that her aunt was to sail on a certain ship and was only prevented from doing so by slipping and breaking her leg on the gangway as she was going on board. The ship went down with all hands. Was this a "special providence"?

Temple replied, "Madam, I did not know your aunt."

★   ★   ★

SOON AFTER THE arrival of his first baby, the farmer's wife went upstairs one evening and found him standing by the cot gazing earnestly into it.

She was very touched by the sight, and tears filled her eyes. Her arm stole softly round him. He started slightly at the touch, and she asked him what he was thinking.

"Nay, lass," he said sadly. "It beats me how they can reckon to ask five pounds for a cot like that."

★   ★   ★

A TRAMP WENT into a pub and asked if he could have some beer if he played the piano for them. The publican said "yes". So he sat down to play.

An old woman sitting in the corner drinking, looked across and saw the tramp had a hole in his trousers. So she went over to him and said: "Do you know there's a hole in your trousers:"

And the tramp said: "No, but no matter; you whistle it and I'll play it."

Down on the Farm

A YOUNG FARM lad was given the task of counting some moor lambs through a smoot in a wall. Sometimes they went rather quickly and the lad got a bit mixed up, but he kept counting.

When they had all passed through he took them into a turnip field where the farmer was busy setting a net.

"Hoo monny hez tha?" the farmer asked.

"Whya," said the lad. "Ah gat a bit muddled. There's either ighty-six or ighty-seven."

"Thoo's gitten t'lot then," said his boss. "There's nobbut ighty-farve when ther all theer."

★　　　★　　　★

A FARMER WHO lives on the moors was limping. He explained: "T'hoss put his foot on mine. It wouldn't have been so bad, but when he put his foot down, he lifted t'other three up."

TWO BILSDALE FARMERS set off to go to Stokesley Mart, one providing the trap and the other the horse. All went well until, coming home, they started arguing and eventually their friendship ended just at the bottom of the then notorious Clay Bank.

The one with the horse jumped out very quickly, unfastened his horse and said: "Ah'll ride mi hoss yam, an' thoo can ride thi trap."

★   ★   ★

JOHN HAD WORKED for nearly sixty years on a Yorkshire farm. One day his employer ventured, gently, to suggest that it was time he retired. The old man was indignant. "Soa it's cummed ti this, 'as it?" he asked. "Ah'm not wanted neer longer? Ah worked for thi grandfather, an' for thi father, an' Ah tell thi, if Ah'd known this here job warn't going to be permanent, Ah'd nivver 'ave takken it on!"

★   ★   ★

FOUR FARMERS WENT to the field by a haunted quarry at dusk to try to catch a dog that was worrying sheep. Peter and Bob were together. Bob was waiting for Peter, who suddenly came running to him, shaking with fear.

"I've seen a man wi'out an head," he gasped.

Bob replied: "Doan't worry, Peter. If he's getten no heead, he can't see thee."

★   ★   ★

"I HEAR TELL that t' 'flu epidemic's ovver i' most parts, but that we've not heard t'end on it yet, like."

"We s'an't hear t' end on it at our house till t' bottle's empty."

"What bottle?"

"Well tha sees, ivver sin' Fred found we'd a drop o' whisky left ovver from Christmas, he's been doin' nowt but ward off t' symptoms."

★   ★   ★

A FAMILY HAD camped for a gloriously fine sunny period at a Dales farm. Each day they had walked miles on fellside and moorland tracks. After the best walk of all, footsore, hot and hungry, they paused at the dairy door to collect their milk, in their elation boasting happily to the farmer's wife of where they had been.

As she handed them their can she completely deflated them by saying: "Ee, what a trail."

"Shep likes to get them into the pen in his own way . . ."

THE FARMER HAD just hired a lad. "An' what shall Ah hev ta do?" said the boy. The farmer looked him up and down. "Do!" he said. "Do! Tha'll hev ta wark, Ah can laik bi misen!"

★   ★   ★

SIXTY YEARS AND more ago, it was a common practice for Dales farmers to have a yearly account with the local blacksmith, which included horse shoeing, repairs to grass cutters, reapers, etc. The arrangement was that the yearly account was rendered at Christmas time, when the black-smith got in a bottle of whisky to keep on the right side of his customers.

"Old Willie", a Dales farmer and Methodist local preacher, went down to pay his account. On settlement, he was offered a glass of whisky.

"Thou knaws I am teetotal," he said to the blacksmith. He pulled a small bottle out of his pocket and said: "If thou doesn't mind, thou can put a drop in the bottle to take home for t'Missus. She's vary dowly, and the Doctor says we haven't to be without a drop of sperret in the house for when she has heart attacks."

It was a Yorkshireman's "Summat for nowt" and it came off.

A DALES SHEPHERD'S employer – a gentleman farmer – was in need of a tup and, much to his shepherd's amazement and anger, decided to trust to his own judgement at the ram sale. The shepherd not only doubted his ability to select an animal most suited to the flock's requirements, but he was vexed at being deprived of his annual visit to the sale, to which came all the shepherds from the surrounding dales.

When his master arrived back with the tup the shepherd viewed it silently and critically from every angle. Finally, after having felt it in the approved style, he stepped back a few paces and asked: "Ye'll hev getten a pedigree wid it?"

"Yes, a very long pedigree," was the reply.

The shepherd threw back his head. "Well," said he, "Ah nivver did see a toop that stood mair in need o' yan."

"I figured they'd be more scared of my wife."

FARMER JOHN WAS disturbed. Something had gone wrong. My aunt, who was staying at the farm asked: "What's the matter with John?"

His wife curtly replied: "He'll just hetta cool down in the seame blood as he got het up in."

★   ★   ★

AN OLD DALES farmer amused his friends at the "local" the other night. It all started when someone asked him how his hens were laying.

"They've all stopped, every one of them," he replied.

"Can you account for it?" asked the landlord.

"I believe I can, Tom," the farmer said. "It's like this. I've been having a small shippon built and the bricklayers have been working on piece-work. I'll swear my hens were listening when them chaps were swanking about the wages they earn laying bricks."

Goods and Services

SOME YEARS AGO, a South Yorkshire farmer, who had a gift for making speeches, was selected by his local Farmers Union branch to attend a big conference in London.

When the time came, his wife packed his bag and he booked into a small hotel in the Metropolis. Before he left home, his wife gave him very strict instructions to leave his bedroom tidy before going out.

On his first night in London, he was required to attend a dinner and introductory meeting at a big hotel. He enjoyed this but when, in due course, he retired to his hotel, he was amazed to see a pair of shoes outside his bedroom door.

He reported this to the night porter, who explained that because the room was so tidy, it had been presumed that the room was vacant.

★ ★ ★

WHEN A LEEDS housewife returned from shopping, her husband asked if she had bought any razor blades.

"No," she said. "You didn't remind me."

"I did – yesterday evening," he replied. "But you may not have heard me. You were asleep in a chair at the time."

A DALES POSTMAN delivered mail to a farm across the river near Hubberholme. During a heavy rainstorm, followed by flood, an access bridge was washed away.

The postman hailed the farmer across the swollen stream and agreed to tie a postcard to a stone and throw it across the raging torrent. Stone and postcard parted company in mid-air and the card floated away on the floodwater. "Nivver mind," shouted the farmer across the roaring water. "Just tell us what wor written on it."

★　　★　　★

IN THE CLOTHING district they relate the story of the Yorkshireman who went to the tailor to buy a new suit. "If I were you," said the tailor, "I'd have two pairs of trousers with the suit."

When the man went to the tailor again, the tailor asked him, "How did you get on with two pairs of trousers?" The man replied: "I thought nowt of 'em; they were too warm."

★　　★　　★

OLD HERBERT SAID to me one day: "Dids't ah ever tell thi' baht that fella as cum fra Bradda (Bradwell)? Is messis wint aht shoppin', an' wen 'er cum back 'er ses – ''as anybody bin?''

'E ses: ''Aye, they'n bin collectin' furst' jumble sale.''

'Er ses: ''Dids't giv 'em owt?''

'E ses: "Aye, ah gev 'em thi mother!"

★　　★　　★

AS I WAS leaving my chiropodist, I passed through the waiting room. An old dear, waiting her turn, looked at me and said: "Nah then, lad, how der yer feel, like a fairy?"

★　　★　　★

TWO SHOPKEEPERS IN a small town appeared outside their shops in the early morning to remove the shutters and sweep the pavement. One called across to the other: "Now, Fred, how is ta?"

"Nothin' much, John," said the other, shaking his head and looking down in the mouth.

"Why? What's ta dew?"

"Why, man, Ah've hed nowt ter eat since yesterday an' tomorrow'll be the third day."

Which after all was a simple way of saying he had not had his breakfast.

A TAILOR WAS delivering his wares when he met a quarryman on his way home from work.

"It's a terrible funny thing," said the quarryman, "but you nivver see a tailor but what he has a few buttons off somewhere!"

"Aye," replied the tailor, "And you nivver see a quarryman but what he has a few slates off!"

★   ★   ★

THE VICAR OF Staincliffe, the Rev. A. Castles, had the degree of M.A. He kept a small herd of cows on the glebeland, employing a youth to do the milking and distribute the milk. This was done from a pony cart on which was an inscription: Rev. A. Castles, M.A. When someone inquired about the meaning of the letters, the lad would say: "They mean 'milk 'awker'."

★   ★   ★

OVERHEARD in a Driffield shop:

Wolds-type gentleman customer: "Thi crabs is dear. Ah can gerrem at arf that price at t'uther shop."

Fishmonger: "Why don't you gerrem there then?"

Customer: "Cos they eh non."

WHILE AWAITING A turn in a Yorkshire shop, a girl about four years old was talking to her mother in a very broad Yorkshire accent.

It was obvious the girl was just learning to count, as when the sales lady pressed the cash register to 20p the little girl said:

"That's a two isn't it, mam?"

To which the mother replied: "No, it's twenty, 'cos there's a nowt on t' end."

* * *

WHEN JACK WAS apprenticed to the trade he was once left in charge of the shop while his master went off for the day. He had to make a frame for a window, and next day his master asked to look at it. Jack produced the frame, and the master gasped.

"Never seen a worse window frame in my life," he said.

"Well, I have," said Jack.

"I'm sure you haven't," said master.

"Look at this one," was the reply, as Jack drew a previous effort from under the bench.

* * *

ONE DAY, AFTER a "difficult" customer had left the shop, I remarked to my employer upon the queerness of some people. "Aye," he said, "They're all queer, except thee and me, and thee's queer sometimes."

* * *

JENNY KEPT A grocer's shop. She was a keen skinflint in many things, but delighted in lavishing finery on her daughter.

Along with sundry jewels and trinkets she bought a gold watch and chain for her daughter. Wishing to have the fact made well-known she would call to her daughter, as a customer entered the shop, "Our Lucy, what o'clock is 't by thy gold watch and thy gold chain?"

* * *

HEARD IN OUR local shop: "The only trouble about being retired from work is that I no longer look forward to Saturday."

A small girl commenting on the number of children on the register at school: "If there were many more few of us, there wouldn't be enough."

Sporting Occasions

DURING THE 1914-1918 War, the legendary Surrey and England cricketer, Jack Hobbs, "guested" for Idle, in the Bradford League. His first appearance attracted a large crowd, and when the great man strode out to the wicket, a hum of excitement spread round the ground.

A young lad opened the bowling for the visitors and, in his very first over, clean-bowled the Master! To his utter amazement the lad heard the Umpire roar: "Not out: stay where you are, Sir" to Jack Hobbs.

The bowler demanded: "You didn't 'no ball' me?"

The Umpire put his hand on the youngster's shoulder and said: "Look lad, all this lot have come to see Jack Hobbs bat, not to see thee bowl him out!"

★　　★　　★

TWO OLD SCHOOL friends of long ago shared the onerous job of organ blowing at our local chapel. To while away the boring hours of sermon time, they would slip quietly downstairs to the choir vestry and play exciting "cricket test matches".

They kept a ball-by-ball score sheet and had an ingenious method of using the individual letters of the hymns for the day, and using a clever code devised by trial and error whereby each letter represented a score or otherwise of each ball and whereby it was possible for their favourite batsman (Herbert Sutcliffe) to score a century or their favourite bowler (Wilfred Rhodes) to take 10 wickets in an innings.

Of course, M.C.C. rules forbade the closure of the match for trifles like the closing hymn and many was the time when a male choir member had to slip out to provide wind for an enraged organist.

★　　★　　★

YOUNG GILLIAN SAT for a while at the cricket match but soon joined a group of other children playing on a nearby heap of sand. Seemingly she had lost all interest in the cricket.

During one innings, the third man in was out first ball.

"By Jove," exclaimed my husband, "he's got a duck."

On arrival home Gillian was asked if she had enjoyed the cricket.

"It was lovely," she answered, "and what do you think, grannie? One man won a duck!"

THE NEW PARSON, being a "new broom", decided to clean the village thoroughly. One bright morning he met Joe, the village poacher, with hands deep in pockets.

"Good morning, Joe," said the parson.

"Good mornin' to ye, parson," said Joe without removing his hands from his coat pockets.

The parson had a notion as to what Joe had in those pockets.

"It would be much more seemly, Joe," said the parson, "if you kept a couple of pigs than those horrible little ferrets!"

"Aye," said Joe, with a twinkle in his eye, "and shouldn't I look a fool goin' rabbitin' wi' a couple of pigs!"

★   ★   ★

I WAS PRESENT at a Test match at Headingley in the early 'thirties, I think, during a West Indian tour. It was a particularly warm afternoon and the cricket degenerated into a slow and unenterprising game.

I was watching immediately below the scoreboard and I, together with the rest of a large crowd, had sunk into a half coma. Suddenly from the street outside, a motor-bus backfired and the loud report echoed over the ground. Immediately a Yorkshire voice at the side of me shouted: "By gow, t'scoorer's shot hissen."

SOME TIME AGO, two miners from the West Riding decided to spend a holiday at a certain hotel a few miles outside Blackpool. Leaving their scarves and whippets at home, they arrived all spick and span at their apartments, and after a bit of introduction settled down to enjoy themselves. The landlord sized them up and decided to do his best towards making them comfortable. He gave them a few ideas as to how they could spend their time, but the usual reply was that they felt lost without their whippets.

As a last resort he suggested a day's trout fishing. Their reply was that they had never done "owt o' t'sort," but they would try it.

So he fit them up with the tackle and directed them to where he thought was the best place, and off they went.

After about an hour's silence, the following dialogue took place –

"Jack!" said one.

"Well?" replied the other.

"Copt owt?"

"Noa!"

Another half hour's silence, then came again: "Jack!"

"Well?" replied the other.

"Copt owt?"

"Noa!"

Another half hour went by, then the same question, and the same answer.

After a while, one of them said: "Ah'll tell thi what, Jack, yon landlord's nooan sich a bad sort of a chap."

Said the other: "Well, he's all reight, but hah's ter meean?"

"Nay. Ah just wondered if they're varry expensive?"

"If what's expensive?" asked the other.

"Them things 'at floats on t'watter, 'cos mine sunk aboon an 'ahr sin'."

J.S. VARLEY.

FRED SUGGESTED THEY should have a day out and try their luck at Doncaster races. Knowing little about form, they decided to pool their resources and back second favourites throughout.

An outsider won the first race, causing them to have doubts about their system.

"We were contemplating doubling our stake on the next race when we caught sight of our local bookie enjoying a busman's holiday. I asked him if he could give us a good tip in the next race. 'Certainly,' he said, 'put all you can on the favourite; it's a cert. I've £50 riding on it.'

"Thanking him, we splashed out most of our money on it. Of course, the second favourite romped home. Our bookie friend was apologetic and gave us another cert to make amends, so we scraped together a fiver and laid it at the best odds. True to form, it never made the first three.

"After this disaster, all we could do was watch the lucky punters collecting their winnings. Feeling peckish, I gave Fred my last quid and asked him to get a meat pie each at the stall. Ten minutes later he came back carrying four bags of crisps. 'What's this?' I said. 'Don't tell me they ran out of pies? I can see they're still selling 'em.'

"'I know,' said Fred, 'I bumped into that know-all bookie again, didn't I!'."

★　　★　　★

ONCE WHEN Mr. "Jim" Lumb, the Elland cricketer, was a professional in Scotland he met Schofield Haigh, also a professional in the land of the Thistle, and heard the story of a cricketer who appealed for l.b.w. "As there was no answer," Haigh said, "I turned round to the umpire. There he was standing up, yet asleep. When I wakened him I shouted, 'I'm appealing for leg before'."

"Did it hit yer leg, Jamie?" asked the umpire.

"Aye," said Jamie.

"Then yer'r oot, Jamie," said the umpire sadly.

★　　★　　★

IT WAS THE Battle of the Roses at Headingley and Yorkshire were put in to bat. The batsman knocked a magnificent six and a little man jumped up and called: "Well played, sir, well played!"

The man beside him said: "Oh, tha cums thro Yorkshire then?" "Oh no," the little man replied.

The very next ball put the batsman out, middle stump. Up jumped the little man again: "Well bowled, sir, well bowled!" "Aw, I see, tha cums thro Lancashire?" "No, I don't come from Lancashire either."

"Then, sit thi'sen down and keep quiet. This 'as nowt to do wi' thee!"

A WIFE SAID to her husband: "Did ta goa fishing o' Setterda, Bill, or did ta goa ta t'Fish Heead Arms?"

"I wor fishing, an' cop't six gurt whoppers," was the reply.

"Nay I thowt hez mitch," observed the wife. "That fishmonger hez med another mistak'. He charged us for eight."

★　　★　　★

BEFORE POLLUTION HAD done its worst, the stream had contained a goodly head of fish of many kinds, but now it was only the optimist who wetted a line. Looking over the bridge, and seeing a stranger wielding a rod, the native shouted: "What's tha fishin for, Mister?" To which question he received the brief and surly reply: "Salmon."

"Salmon," repeated the man on the bridge, "there ain't no salmon in these parts!"

Came the even more surly reply: "There ain't any fish at all – so I might as well fish for salmon as ought else!"

★　　★　　★

MY FRIEND WAS at Scarborough watching the cricket on the day when Hutton hit up a fantastic score. He could score off anything they sent along and hit the bowling unmercifully.

Behind him were four young fellows, keen cricketers.

One remarked: "I've been told that Hutton's eyesight is going."

At once another said: "Gosh! Then he must have a darned good *smell.*"

★　　★　　★

A FISHING PARTY from a Leeds Club went to Ulleskelf for their day's outing, repairing afterwards to the "Fisherman's Arms", where a meal was to be had for a shilling per head.

On this particular day the anglers were in good eating fettle and the old landlord kept wandering up and down the room and wondering if they would ever finish. At last he could stand it no longer and asked: "Where do ye boys come fra?" "Leeds," they cried with one voice. "By gow," said the landlord, "but you can't arf eat."

The following week another party was going from the same club to Ulleskelf, and fearing that the landlord might set out to ration them, they agreed to say they came from Wakefield. Sure enough as the meal progressed the landlord started his wanderings. Curiosity getting the better of him, he enquired what was their home town.

"Wakefield," they cried. The old man studied them for a while and then said: "By gow, but you eat like Leedsers."

A YORKSHIRE GAMEKEEPER was discussing a day's shoot with some friends and also his difficulty in finding the proper title for one of the guests, a bishop.

"I noar reet well that a lord or a herl I calls 'im lord, and a dook 'yer grace', but t'bishop fair bested me. I wer standin' near 'im, and up jumps a rabbit. I shouts out, 'Shoot the little devil yer 'Oliness!' But I could see by t'expression on 'is face I war wrong."

★   ★   ★

AT THE (OTLEY) rugby match the other Saturday, two veteran supporters had their own views on a decision of the referee. "Of course he wor offside," yelled one. "How could he be?" retorted the other. All their knowledge of the rules of the game was brought to bear in the ensuing argument.

Finally, having had enough, the second came in with: "Alreet, then, thou sez he wor offside and Ah doan't reckon he wor, so us'll agree to differ, that's all."

"Oh no we woan't," came the emphatic rejoinder. "Ah'm not differing wi ye, 'cos Ah knoas Ah'm reet."